QUICKENING FIELDS

PATTIANN ROGERS

QUICKENING FIELDS

PENGUIN POETS

PENGUIN BOOKS

An imprint of Penguin Random House LLC
375 Hudson Street
New York, New York 10014
penguin.com

LIBRARY OF CONGRESS CATALOGING-IN-PUBLICATION DATA
Names: Rogers, Pattiann, 1940- author.
Title: Quickening fields / Pattiann Rogers.
Description: First edition. | New York : Penguin Books, [2017] | Series:
    Penguin poets
Identifiers: LCCN 2016053786 | ISBN 9780143131328 (softcover)
Subjects: | BISAC: POETRY / American / General.
Classification: LCC PS3568.O454 A6 2017 | DDC 811/.54—dc23 LC record
available at https://lccn.loc.gov/2016053786

Printed in the United States of America
10 9 8 7 6 5 4 3 2 1

Set in Fournier MT Std
Designed by Elyse Strongin, Neuwirth & Associates

For our early ancestors who first recognized
these virtues, who then created names for them and
passed the thought of each to their children and to us:
honesty, compassion, generosity, forgiveness,
justice, loyalty, love.

CONTENTS

ONE

The Older Kid   3

Coming Back   5

Keeping the Body Warm   7

Rumors of Snow, Christmas Eve   9

Winter Camping   11

Faith and Certainty: Arctic Circles   13

Inheriting the Earth   15

TWO

Forth into View, Random Warriors   19

Finding the Cat in a Spring Field at Midnight   21

Noonday and a Deep Idea of Yellow   22

The Word (Sun After Rain)   23

The Woodland Snail at Twilight   24

The Congregating of Stars   26

The Estate of Solemnity   28

THREE

Musical and Motoring Cycles   31

Young Summer Sating   33

Harvest Tale   35

Grand Sky/Grand Prairie   36

I Thought I Heard a White-Haired Man with a Purple Tie
    Say, "The Mind Creates What It Perceives."   38

Capturing a Wild Pony   40

The Thing in Itself   42

FOUR

Waking God at Dawn   47

Seeing the God Statement   48

The Imagination Imagines Itself to Be a God   50

Gospel   51

Easter Frogs   52

The God of Sunday Evening, June 7, 1987   54

This Is Not About God   55

FIVE

Grandmother's Sister   59

Receiving Prayers   61

The Moss Method   62

The Most Primitive Peace   63

The Art of Imitation   65

The Highest Octaves of Light: A Canticle   66

Crux   68

SIX

Seven Variations on Redefinition

    1. Accommodation   73

    2. Predestination   74

    3. Six Reasonable Compositions   76

4. Fire in Freedom   77

5. The Idea of Zero on a Moonless Night   79

6. The Five Dog Saga   81

7. Playroom: The Visionaries   83

SEVEN

The Abandonment   87

Earth-Night Errors   88

Next to Sleep   90

Particular Falls   91

Calling to Measure   93

Statement Preliminary to the Invention of Solace   95

EIGHT

Pursuing the Study of a Particular Reality   99

Is Knowledge of the Universe Holy?   101

How the Old See Death   103

Taking Leave   105

Death Vision   107

Notes   *111*

Acknowledgments   *113*

QUICKENING FIELDS

ONE

He moves deftly along sandhills, balances
on the spurred and spiny branches
of the honey mesquite, enters each bud nip,
goes clear to the sweetish pulp of the bean-like
seeds and back again.

Weaving among the grey down-feathers
on the edges of the loon's open eye, he pauses,
peers into the center of that red-black
ball, more velvet, more roiling than the sun.

He descends and descends, just as surely,
into the ocean, reaches, enters the tunnel
of the warm water worm on the bottom, slips
into that sheath of skin, reverses, rises,
slides beneath the sea robin, skims as he passes
the burbot and goosefish, the rat-tail,
on his way back up rides the remora
on the ride of the shark, keeps in the kite-like
shadow of the manta ray.

He crosses barefoot every delineation
of black and white—the stripes of polecat,
badger and Grevy's zebra, the wider swaths
of penguin, tapir, the narrow-barred wings
of Indian swallowtail, black tit, banded
broadbill. He moves through each sun-and-shadow
slat between bobcat and cottontail, measures
by paces all the several fractions of the moon.

After traversing the gypsum dunes and the upper
bajada, after winding to the bottom
of the chia, the ringstem and the peyote rose,

he stops, checks his odometer, his quasar
timepiece, his depth gauge, looks back to see
who's keeping up.

I could choose to follow
a leader like that.

Whenever she comes home,
it's always easy to guess where she's been.

If she comes back racing, her hair
and trousers wet with salty dew, petals
and pollen from purple monkshood and angelweed
clinging to her bare feet, she's been chasing
the caribou, following their mossy antlers
through the tundra foliage along the cliffs
by the sea.

If she comes slowly home at midnight trailing
narrow scarves of pale silk, her hair
pulled back from her white powdered face,
her silver eyelids closed, she has been
beside the ice-covered lake in the clearing
learning to see the snowy winter moon
exactly as frozen water sees it.

And if she returns by running uphill backwards,
her shadow preceding her, then she has accompanied
the humpbacked salmon down to the sea
and back again, thrashing through fierce forward currents,
ruffling stones, following the two directions
death faces, all the way down and back again.

But if she comes home like dawn comes
to the forest being gradually filled
by the quickened moth, the twitch of the glancing
lizard and the oak-branched sun of its own presence,
if she returns like light returns to the flame
of a single candle burning in a darkening dusk,
if she comes, moving the way a slender

spring laurel moves as it travels from its damp
roots into the pure white spaces of its heart,
then everyone knows for certain
who it is she's been to visit,
what she heard while she was there.

1.

We have been forced by cold winds
bearing across briar-covered fields, up craggy
gulleys, through every rock crack and tree-lined
crevice, to cover the body perfectly from the beginning.
Fitting wool to the chest, we have been compelled to learn
how to create the idea of one thing in the medium of another—
the transference of shape, the abstraction in cloth
of rib cage and sternum.

Knees and thighs in motion over icy creeks
and slick boulders must be studied carefully
to make the snow leggings functional. The essence of foot
must be perceived first in order to perfect the fur-lined boot,
and the boot more than copies the foot. Slipped into place,
it redefines capabilities.

What is it we learn of the hand
when we see its image over and over
in the empty leather glove? What is it we learn from leather
when we see its imitation of fingers? Maybe the glove
is simply proof of our ability to invent
and give form to a notion.

In the early dark chill of that first concentrated attempt
to match the pattern of the sleeve
to the free motion of the arm
something else of significance must have been discovered.

2.

I wish you had just come through the door
of this room from outside. I wish your body were cold
and shivering, as if you'd just crossed a two-mile-long white

winter field, its tree-line dark and purple and blowing
with heavy evening snow.

Then I could take the icy scarf from around your neck
and brush the frozen drops from your hair and taste
the cold-rain flavor on your face, and I could notice again
the distinct determination of the body to exist.

And I could rub each of your toes and suck your fingertips
and, in its shell-like iciness against my cheek, remember
the aloof vulnerability of the ear. I could find
fine quilts of down and thick woven cotton
and put you to bed with pillows by the fire and pull
blankets to your chin and remember again your chin.

And my own body being warm all along,
I could get into bed and lie down close to you
under the blankets to help out—my legs around yours,
your belly against mine, everything you have—
all night together in wonder that there could be
such joy as loving bodies to keep warm.

The snow must be somewhere waiting in the heavens,
far above the definite point of light where the eye
stops seeing. It is said that stars pass easily
through its white gauze girth as it falls from that height,
and when it settles over broken fields and frozen lakes,
the vacant marks made by the constellations
can still be seen in its solid lay.

Maybe the snow waits, curved perfectly
over the earth, the silent white side of night,
hovering with all the power and promise of a savior
who hasn't yet descended.

It is rumored that snow fashions,
as it falls, a definite white storm in the distance
of its coming, slowly descending on the bare backs of ponies,
stripped sycamores, the branches of naked willows,
with the only kind of motion angels ever crave.

Some people plan to run outdoors naked
into the storm's first signs, believing each flake heals
the body like a savior as it touches flesh. Some say
that eyes which have fashioned the six sides of themselves
will be the first to see the first signs of snow.

Maybe there are eyes that can fashion themselves to see
naked angels quivering on the bare backs of ponies,
definite points of light descending to touch
the first signs of naked flesh. Or maybe it is only
waiting angels who can see inside the distance of themselves
constellations in a savior of snow, the naked backs

of ponies touched by stars, redemption in the motion
of snow slowly turning the night inside out.

Father, this is our prayer tonight:
wherever healing power exists, in a star of ice
waiting somewhere in the distant heavens or in eyes
fashioned to perceive that rumor, may a snowy storm
of angels come quickly, touching all those waiting naked
for such a promised savior.

He rises suddenly, naked
and white out of the mountain
drifts, or else he slides
in one motion from the broken
sea onto the ice edge of my bed,
dripping salt water. How can I
remember exactly?

Upon me—one long moaning sigh
from his lips under my gown,
and I'm stopped with ice from throat
to knees. His mouth, moving slowly
down the back of my neck, sizzles
with subzero burns. His fondling
blue fingers tingle six-sided
crystals along my breasts.

And yet his moon-grey eyes when open
shine on me like light below
the horizon shines on solid grey
seas below grey clouds.

He's the guttural growl of a white
arctic fox, a froth of white ptarmigan
smothering against my face, pervasive
as the inside out of a black polar night,
a white raven circling, making black
beakings on my belly. A snow hare,
he crouches at my knees, his white mustache
maddening as he nips frost-bites
around my thighs.

He's the hood of a snowy owl, a white
cowl, a mute monk. Sucking his earlobe
is like taking a burning pod of frozen
white wine into my mouth.

If only he had deep drapes of snow-laced
fur like the musk ox to cover, to hide us both,
it might be possible to encourage more.

Shivering, I make a dark snow
angel on the bed as he indicates,
while his advancements rise, swirling
at my hips—then the blizzard blindness,
the stream of sleety stars.

But all in all, his frozen
body—the gaping spires and frigid
temple winds, the icy amnesias—pressed hard
against me tonight is the only way
I have to understand every warm bud
and pocket-protected spring
I previously cherished
and called my own.

It takes one part of one and another
of the other to understand how she shifts
and turns slowly over now, rattling, mewing,
chomping her black lips in her sleep,
adjusting her bulk within the snow-covered
den dug to the permafrost.

It requires one part of each to assert
that she is oblivious, yet aware,
of the two naked, womb-sleek cubs, eyes
sealed shut, smothering, jerking,
butting again, believing wholeheartedly
in the paps they find by feel in the rich
fat of her presence.

It is necessary to possess a certain
confidence in order to state that she stalks
at this moment a calculable distance
from the Pole over floes of ice above
the dark salt-depths within which a bevy
of hair seals, unaware of her furred feet
on the crust above, weave, interweave,
backside, bellyside, in truth,
never witnessed by any of us.

It is written, and many agree, that each
transparent tubular hair of her white fur
dumbly directs shafts of dim sunlight
warmth down to her absorbing black hide.

Though some may doubt the rare religious
paw prints she leaves on the snowy plains, still
it might be claimed as a certainty that she lopes along,
pauses, woofs with her nose raised, scenting,

it is surmised, walrus, whale carcass, as she circles
back again beneath the shadow of a tracking
helicopter overhead now ascending, now banking left,
now, with camera and crew, in fact, we are told,
heading home.

We were ancient then in our youth.
We journeyed often to the great plateau
of ice, a desert of white under the sky
from one horizon to the other out of sight.
We stood like trees at the edge, shaggy,
still, watching.

That noble shining, a steady continent
of white, like blindness, its breath the easy
falling form of clouds on the horizon.
Many of us watched it breathe, the merest
motion maintaining the grace of possibility.

We were glorified by the beauty, icefalls,
valley bends, firn snow solid as alabaster
in shapes like statues of creatures—white bear
and fox, the wings of owl, stare of rabbit—
all stopped by ice in figures of dance.

Once we saw a savior hung from crystal
spears, and we prayed to that celestial
glory, though our prayers were ignored
with an indifference we knew was wisdom.

We often heard the ice speaking in low
lamentations or humming in alternating tones,
like stones rubbing against each other
underwater, sometimes a sporadic music,
high-pitched like birds screeching in rapture,
frantic and lost. The terror was majestic.

We chanted the words we heard it speak
and were transformed by the sound
of its own utterances, sometimes comforted,
sometimes enraged to violence by its
tortured harshness.

Occasionally when the sun first appeared
at dawn, spirits rose like gossamer angels
from this great white body that was ours,
swayed, rose, and flew away. We swayed
like those spirits, imitating their motions.
Yet none of us ever flew away.

Nothing about this magnificence was shallow.
Once, along its farthest horizon, it shattered
and split apart, the roar of the shattering
breaking our sleep, shuddering the land.
Those who journeyed to that crevasse afterward
looked down into the vanishing blue depth
of its presence, the darkening temple within,
its corridors and hallways. It lay open, spread
like arms open in offering, a lover lying
open in offering. We lowered our dead
into that temple, and they were taken.

No one knew this world as we knew it.
We marked its voluptuous emptiness,
a heaven of solidity, a virginity of white.
We began to savor the taste of a morning
breeze coming over newly fallen snow,
to long for the lift of glacial light at dawn
bestowing a mirage of redemption.

And at night in our sleep, we achieved
our dreams, becoming the shadows of clouds
flowing over the frozen architecture
of our deity as if over the moon, slipping
into its white fissures and dells, our bodies
as intimately close to every divination of living
ice as perfection and human could ever be.

TWO

The slender checkered beetle, pale
earth brown, sallies forth from among
the bark canals of the oak, the eaten mar
of the woody gall left dying. Her spiny
yellow hairs sparkle in the summer sun.

Lacewings, locust, and laurel loosen
cocoon, carapace, and bud, shimmy out
and pause, airing wings expanding like rumpled
petals, spreading petals opening like slatted
wings, as they pass into the new world.

Toe by toe the children of the sun depart
from the east out of living fire to become
spikes, glumes, anthers, sheaves, broad
montane grassland, flowing steppe,
savannah, veld, wild horse pampas.

The fiddler crab with his royal blue
spot emerges beside the great charging
dawn of the morning sea, scuttles sideways
out of the drenched sands and savory
mud bank of the tidal marsh.

Now echoes in cougar lairs, snake crannies,
coon burrows, the hillside den of grey fox.
Moonrat's nose appears from the crevice
in the bluff, sniffing fish and wormy mud.
Turtle's beak shows at shell's edge first.
Claws and feet extend directly.

The smooth, golden-green swale
of the trout swivels upward, breaks
through the boundaries of sky
with its mouth wide open gulping day.

After parting the flap, after gripping
the knob, after unlatching the gate, after
kicking the door until the hinges crack
and fail and the hindrance falls, then the jaunt,
the saunter, the sprint, the lope, the totter,
ramble and meander, the traipse and slink,
the shamble, shuffle, gallop and glide,
the push against the beyond begins.

It takes a peculiar vision to be able to detect
precisely where

the field grasses brushed by blowing
stars and the odor of spring
in the breath of sweet clover buds
and the star-mingled calls of the toads
in the threading grasses and the paws
of the clover brushing through the field
of stars and the star-shaped crickets
in the ears of the sweet grasses
and the tail of the night flicking
through the calls of the clover and the spring
stars slinking past the eyes of midnight
and the hour of the field mouse passing
through the claws of the stars and the brushing
haunches of the weeds and starry grasses
threading through the eyes of the mouse
and the buds of the stars calling
with the sweet breath of the field

end
and the cat begins.

How far down does the yellow of the sunflower
descend? By intention, mayhem, or godsend,
how deep do the reverberations of that glowing
yellow go, through stem and viney roots, into the night
of the loamy soil, into the buried crystal of yesterday's
rain, then rising back up and out again into pollen
and petal and up deep into the fiery blue/orange sky
of the sun's yellow summer eye? I wonder about this.

And does the spirit of yellow in a meadowlark's
feathers pass down through each of their central shafts
into vein and bone marrow, into the thunderous cells
of that tiny bird heart, deep into genetic tremor,
concept and source, then back up into the pure black
eye seeking yellow in the world, spying the twitch
in the dull yellow rump of the female nearby?
Would his song be yellow if sound could be seen?

It's merely a color, afterall, without substance,
an airy stripe in the spectrum, one angle of a glint
of spectral light. Maybe yellow in the arc of the first
rainbow that formed over earth was the first birth
of yellow in that foreign time with no names.

The deepest yellow might be the yellow in the eyes
of that coyote watching me from across the field. I see
his eyes, perceive their yellow, the thrum of a primeval
chord. I match and return the charm of his wily, wicked,
essential will to live, the same as mine. Two yellows
multiplied deep in calculation.

Yellow wing dragonfly, yellow-headed blackbird,
goldfinch, swallowtail, buttercup, downy yellow
violet, "Mary . . . hair of gold and lips like cherries,"
sunsap apple, yellow tourmaline . . . I'm with you all
today, deep, deep into yellow-surmising.

A rustling shower passes, and now fiery suns
as small as seeds hang suspended on the point-
tips of every spear of forest pine.

Galaxies,
I say, and a wraith appears, an actual apparition
of bestowing beside me in the glittering forest.
I know it.

Prayer in the shape of the wind rises.
Galaxies fly, a rain of galaxies in motion, a ringing
crescendo of light.

Who is it who makes music
with falling stars of water? Who is it who tunes
the art of benevolence?

Is it burning water
that creates rainlight in falling pellets of sun?
Is it sunlight that creates the voice of galactic
rains?

All of those deaf suns are singing in chorus
together: *This is so.*

The snail, *Helix hortensis*, being multi-dimensional,
touches in any moment many more things than one.
The mucous tongue of his single foot,
as sensitive as a bloom of honeysuckle, licks,
probes each bump and fissure of the fallen
hickory twig. And while the polish
of his stone back, between clouds and shadows,
assumes the light of the dawning Alpha Centauri,
the crude eye of his tentacle tip seeks and becomes
one with the emerging blue point of Jupiter.

Brother to the temperate forest floor,
he touches also, by kinship, the snail that touches
the snail that sleeps in ice above the snowline
of the Himalayas, and he is bound by blood
to the conical, creamy white snail
that pulls over desert dust to shelter
in gold Chihuahua flax.

He is cousin to cuttlefish, paper nautilus,
blue-ringed octopus, and the cowrie *Volva volva*,
likewise related to pearl mussel, spiny
oyster, naked sea butterfly and otter shell.
He has claim therefore to intimacy
with the eight webbed coordinates of the sea,
the rock hinges and latches of the will,
jeweled hearts, the gliding nude bodies
of all ocean angels.

The embodiment of abstraction, he is made kin
to wavering underwater sun by the undulating
thrust of his own locomotion. By his body parts
having twisted 180 degrees in the egg,
he has experienced every inverted aspect

of *above* and *below*, *within* and *without*,
and he has essential knowledge of *left*,
for his shell opens always to the *right*.

He has touched even the inner stem
of the human brain, for he alone gives rise
to the slow caravan of self-sufficiency
of snail dreams.

Now he is concentrating the meteorological
elements of the evening in his damp, weighty
moment-of-body in the palm of my hand,
held in the vise of my attention.
See how he touches me and the one beyond
me at my shoulder and the one beyond
the one beyond . . .

Watch now and be alert. What foundations
are jarred, what histories shaken
by the beginning turn and stretch
of his four horns, the advancing quiver
of his tilting case?

They often meet in mountain lakes,
no matter how remote, no matter how deep
down and far they must stream to arrive,
navigating between the steep, vertical piles
of broken limestone and chert, through shattered
trees and dry bushes bent low by winter,
across ravines cut by roaring avalanches
of boulders and ripping ice.

Silently, the stars have assembled
on the surface of this lost lake tonight,
arranged themselves to match the patterns
they maintain in the highest spheres
of the surrounding sky.

And they continue on, passing through
the smooth, black countenance of the lake,
through that mirror of themselves, down through
the icy waters to touch the perfect bottom
stillness of the invisible life and death existing
in the nether of those depths.

Sky bound—yet touching every needle
in the torn and sturdy forest, every stone,
sharp, cracked along the ragged shore—the stars
appear the same as in ancient human ages
on the currents of the old seas and the darkened
trails of desert dunes, Orion's belt the same
as it shone in Galileo's eye, Polaris certain above
the sails of every mariner's voyage. An echoing
light from the Magi's star, that beacon, might even
be shining on this lake tonight, unrecognized.

The stars are congregating, perhaps
in celebration, passing through their own
names and legends, through fogs, airs,
and thunders, the vapors of winter frost
and summer pollens. They are ancestors
of transfiguration, intimate with all the eyes
of the night. What can they know?

By right, it reigns in its places—in long beards
of Spanish moss hanging from a live oak
on a windless evening, and in the chill of new
icicles rigidly, imperceptibly lengthening. Cavern
stalagmites are almost majestic with solemnity.

Undeviating focus is solemn too, as in the toad's
steady study of a wisp of insect whirring closer,
in the diver's pause at the edge of the board just before
the push away, in the suspended, final note of a requiem.

The black morel and the tree ear mushroom
are solemn without grief, solemn without joy,
solemn without reverence, without a single
flicker of green or lift of a wing or cry.

The solitary seed in the dark sunless center
of a peach or plum, with all of its promise intact,
is the perfect embodiment of solemnity.

But the most solemn, most stalwart, the least
wavering are the tors and crags, the towering desert
spires and carved pinnacles, the devoted ascents
and sharp, raw rims of boulders and bluffs, the maw
of a distant cave I saw yesterday and the day before,
and the grave echo there of the *day* and the *before*.

Mystics and divines have always sought the pure,
white-rock serenity of the silent, solemn moon
bound in its flight alone far above the peaks, far
above the earth, surrounded there forever by bevies
of giddy stars, all asparkling, all aglow.

THREE

Both have circles that span the globe,
a certain clockwork movement that spins
the countryside. They hold this in common
with each other and the stars.

Like roads, neither can exist without motion,
the interchanges of mingling tones and time,
whether traveling through the purple/auburn trills
and dirges of failing autumn plains or in the sudden
flights and treble falls of canyon landscapes.
I can see the scores of broken rock arpeggios
rising and descending in the distance.

Who will say that the swelling and flickering
lights of city streets, the harrow of grate
steam rising, the flash of chrome, cymbal
or brass, all witnessed as one rolls along,
that these have neither cadence nor coda?

And who will claim that chords and cadenzas
do not possess momentum with many wheels
turning inside their own branching sequences
of light, those measures resembling in resonance
the shadows of winter sycamores and oaks lining
the way, imitating in form the rumble rhythm
of a bridge, its open steel beams crossing over
and past one another, as perfect in their timing
as partners in a dance?

Once, traveling the edge of coastal cliffs, I heard
in raucous meter and percussion the epic theme
of earth-and-ocean wars I saw raging below.

Does the pace of our motoring, the pressures
of increasing and waning acceleration, make
the music of our journeys? Or does music create

the motif we hear repeated in a ritual forest
of pines sedately standing by, in the wheezing
and widening harmonic net of birds wheeling
to escape, tall seeded grasses showing their white
sun-sides in unison blown by the rush of the passing?

Although we allow our musical and motoring
creations to carry us, we can rarely distinguish
within their cycles which destination
is a beginning, which beginning a finale.

We could hear that first summer coming,
sounding low like heralding drums rumbling
far away, like a desert freshet, like a torrent
of rain all-enveloping, cascading down
a stone-dry arroyo unstoppable.

Some of us witnessed it coming in random
dynamics through the distance, the spinning
bowls and rolling barrels of its hot brasses
glinting among the cloud shadows on the plains
and on into the darker buddings of the forest.

And we felt the sound of sun sprouting,
pushing and parting bindings of sizzling
spear grasses and teffs, an airy swarm
of midges, scattered lacewings, checkered
whites, bee breath everywhere, the hard
beginnings of pomes and pips. We heard
the vines, already smothering, bosky
pea bush, rabbit brush, snakeweed flowering
one after the other, all repeating their chords
of climbing blossoms, blinding the ears.

Prairie swallows, kingbirds, blackbirds, larks
swirled and darted over the flows of the land,
sounding their triangular notes into the delves,
attacking and courting, frantic with purpose.
We believed in light and its patterns of power.

The fragrance of this new born summer
was the purest force, rank, sweet, meaty,
and rotten, heady powder, lilac talc, one brief
dusting of paprika-pepper plucking like a guitar
barely there, a remembrance of cinnamon.

That first summer came suffocating
with temptations of pain, not ardor, though
we called the ardor pain, the way it could take
anyone unwillingly and the body had to move,
to run to catch up, the allure, once a cry, once
the terror of laughter (a singer everywhere
singing an encore in solo), to follow, finally
grasping, swinging over, lifted, carried away,
every faith in the body holding on.

One night between the black sky and the golden
land (thrice golden at evening—wheat fields
with their wind-waves of copper grasses and blades,
spinning reapers and threshers, and bronze boys
bold with light); one night between the black

furrows of his body and the gold of his hands,
we were curled tight around each other as if inside
the black spiral of a fossil conch harboring its own
ocean pulse, the same surge and sea-rolling motion
flowing through the fields in the black swirl of the sky;

like two bees, our fur black and golden, we were buried
in the flume of summer gold, kept by an angel of gold
blessings and black amens slipping over us like morning,
wings and a half-mask, a halo of black, a hum of gold.
Like stars our bodies were multiple against a black

sky in that full harvest, each a repose, each an urgency.
Black drums were rumbling low, his breath at my ear,
at my breasts. He was the ripeness of wheat, tasting of sun,
the bursting of sun redolent with seeds, both of us fingering,
inside and out, our shining tangle of golden strings.

Both harbor the vastness of space. One holds the space
of starlight, thunder snow, rock and icy comets, scrolls
of clouds; the other the spaces inside seed heart and ovum,
root webs, spider webs, budded blossoms.

They lean together tightly day and night, pressing
one into the other, each creating the horizon of the other.
They exchange themselves. At evening one becomes
the steady night in which the other lives. Yet witness
how the moon first rises from the body of the prairie
into the height of the sky that then possesses it.
Their horizons are persistent illusion.

They give and they borrow. The sky can be balmy
with prairie fragrances—primrose, sweet clover, sage,
and wild strawberry, mint, first frost dusting dry grasses,
spent sedges and forbs.

And by the *chit-seeee* of finches, the flutey calls
of meadowlarks, wooing doves, coyote screeches,
the purring of great plains toads, barking of short-
eared owls . . . the sky has voice.

Yet everything prairie-born—scurf pea, hawkweed,
shrike, deer mouse, switch grass, pronghorn—arrives
given life by the breath of the sky, bounty bestowed
from the sky of rain.

Blue flax, winged dock, asters, random clusters
of lupine and phlox—every flower of prairie flora
imitates the same succulent simmer as the night-
filled simmer of their sister stars.

Inseparable, these two partner with the dawning
sun in the irresistible, mad dance of morning, easy
moving currents of willows and flashing grasses,

insects floating like glassy filaments, the rustling
slither to a basking rock, a dart upward far away,
perfumed pollen powder airborne and descending,
all life linked to earth, all life shining like the sky.

I THOUGHT I HEARD A WHITE-HAIRED MAN WITH A PURPLE TIE SAY, "THE MIND CREATES WHAT IT PERCEIVES."

I stand facing the field-pond, my back
to a broad, low hill of cropped grasses, my back
to a line of ragged dead brush stacked
after the field-clearing, my back to the summer sun
at eye-level (were my eyes turned westward),
my back to three mares
grazing leisurely on the low rise.

Or my back may be turned
to a colorless, blank non-existence
beginning its nothingness at the peripheral edges
of my senses, a sterile emptiness pressing
against me full length—thighs, inner knees,
scalp, neckbones. How can the back
be brave enough to confront continuously
such a possible void?

Maybe I too stand at someone's back,
the details of my presence here as I stare
at the damselflies above the pond, as I imagine the horses
shifting their rumps in the sun, being the subject
of someone else's hypothesis.

But why should what I call the youngest mare
seem to emerge now out of that postulated space at my back,
created first, I suppose, by my ears giving her approach
a rock-clashing of hooves? She nudges me, and I guess
the knowledge of my arm is making her insistent, green-flecked
muzzle real, her grass-interpreted lips and snout actual.
I think she pushes against my ribs, passing me once
with the stinging sweep of her tail, then turning back.
And even given plenty of room, she crowds closer,
side-swiping me again, her warm hip knocking hard

against my shoulder until she turns and saunters
three steps into the pond and lies down suddenly
rolling at my feet, moss-thick waves of mud sloshing
over the bank, splattering my legs. (I am creating quickly now.)
The awesome girth of her whole great belly is wet
and foamy, fully exposed in my plain sight, and I see
the flashing metal of her upturned hooves, and I hear
the sweet sucking sound of the water and the shrieking
exit of the killdeer. Surely my own sharp cry in my ears
and hers is enough to make something definite of her being
as she rises, dripping with mud, to stare at me again head-on.

Mare, here is a gift to carry in that eternal blind
spot of your own that lies between the tops
of your spade-shaped ears. I give you *this*
as proof of the success of your plot
to assure your own creation this afternoon,
this contrivance of mine
plotting also to emerge from some emptiness,
almost jealous of the shocking success of a body-shaking
haunch, a naked belly, those silver hooves.

Even if it seems the entire expanse
of that prairie is still and empty,
possessing only the unequivocating
flat calm of its study; even if the featureless
swell of the sky remains unbroken,
pressing its blank edges
to the undifferentiated edges
of the encircling plains;
even if the wild canaries
in the brushy thickets continue
their hidden brooding undisturbed
and the savannah sparrows in the weeds
are never frightened nor flushed
and the mud bank of the pond
is only marked by the prints
of cooter and vole, still,
it isn't hard to be convinced
he is there.

One need only squat near the big
bluestem grasses and begin to study
their lead-grey leaves at the roots
to know he has raised his head
from his grazing, and one must simply
continue to examine the spore-powdered
gills of the purple mushroom and count
the larva tunnels of the robber flies
in the dirt, to be confident he is turning,
looking this way. It is only necessary
to remain engaged, memorizing the design
of the corn snake, the thrust
of the spur-throated grasshopper
to be aware that he is *compelled* to come,
must move closer; only necessary

to stare as before, diligently
in the opposite direction, into the distant
horizon of needle grass, into the night
stars farthest from him, remaining
indifferent to everything except the details
composing his absence, in order to hear
the step of his approaching hooves,
to smell the strengthening odor
of his rubbing haunches, to believe
the shadow of his breast moves
nearer over the dust.

It is essential then simply to reach,
without looking, without rising,
over one's shoulder, forgetting
the feel of his nudging snout
at the ribs, ignoring the shiver
of his neck and mane beneath the fingers,
denying out loud to everyone the wonder
of his shimmering muscles beneath
the hand, in order to keep him
forever.

Kioka believes in the universal horse which alone
has given substance and spirit to all fact.

It is from the universal horse that brown leaf-ponies
have learned in autumn how to press and harry
one another, how to part and gather again, pushing
frantically across the lawn, raising dust in their rush
and veer down the dirt road.

And the accumulated rocks comprising the great heights
of the forested mountains to the west are simply
all the inverted stone hoofprints made long ago
by the timeless pony as it galloped back and forth
over the antediluvian plains of the ancient earth.

The alert vacancy of late winter is the pause,
the hesitation of the universal horse at the precipice,
that space of contemplation, too pure and distant
to freeze, held in the white of its eyes as it stammers
and blows thin frost, as it wheels and rears
to gallop away like spring in the opposite direction.

And language simply breaks apart and categorizes
the total horse experience—"seaweed tangled
like a long mane in the salt-wet wind," "sunlight
standing like slender dozing ponies in the shade
of summer poplars," "fog pervading tall weeds
and grasses like the ghost of a stallion dreaming
of the consuming motions of its mating
in the field."

Sex, as Kioka knows it in undefiled darkness,
is the universal horse nuzzling and breathing
at the crotch, its soft snout nudging
and nipping at the crotch.

And the sound of heavenly infinity is the wildness
of that horse, and the heaven in the ceremony
of passion is the domesticity of that horse.
Without the brilliant substance and spirit
of the continuous horse, how could the moon
have adapted itself so well to the limitations
of its own silver stakes and tethers?

The universal horse, undiscovered, is not universal.
Kioka, without discovering his belief
in the universal horse, is not universal master.

Imagine how he must mount then, clinging
and reining, both the one borne and the one leading,
the one carried and the one guiding, whipping
and caressing, approaching the widest ravine,
all stars above and all stars below, now the ledge,
now the maw coming into view; and remember
during the crisis of the ride (Doesn't everyone
know?) how it is the urging stride of his words
spoken in the language of galloping hooves
over the earth that gives all fact and all substance
and all success to that lonely leap.

FOUR

This is the steady shell, as dark as bone,
that has always determined his sleeping.
This is the full notion that becomes the flesh
of his body and the thought that is the measure
of his breath. And this is the statement
that constitutes his rest, as easy and lulling
as the wings of shining insects afloat, as the fading
haunches of thin stars shifting in the late
night grasses of his sleep.

This motion, which intends to imitate here
the early morning gathering of water from sheer
lake-fog to the tip of each beach burr, is the actuality
tracing through his veins like blood.

And *now* is the first streak of light coming
between firmament and heaven, the quick flashing
division of the deep passing suddenly between thick branches,
out of black water and clouds, creating this moment
just before his closed eyes begin to open.

And this is the dream which is urging him to wake,
which presses itself to his vision like a pale leaf
floating on a morning pond, like a sleeping
forehead presses itself against a deepening sky,
the dream which becomes the careful ear
of its own whisper, which becomes the shudder
in the body of its word, the kiss discovering his cheek
moving as lightly as a teal lifting over new
grey marshes, the dream that imagines itself to be
the first object in which he clearly sees himself
rising on one elbow in the wide sun
of his complete waking.

Suppose the statement *Blessed*
are the pure in heart, for they shall see
God were placed like a wreath of violets,
lilies, laurel, and olive, blossoms strung together
like words in a sentence, a garland
launched, set out on a flowing creek.

Imagine that wreath carried
down the frothy rapids, tossed, floating,
slipping over water-smoothed, moss-colored
boulders, in and out of slow, dark pools,
through poplar and willow shadows. It dips,
sinks momentarily, emerges, travels, maintains
its ring, its declaration and syntax.

At times it widens in a broad, deep
current, makes sense as a gift.
The pure become inclusive, spatial,
generous. God and heart are two
spread wings of one open reading.

And at times it narrows, restricts.
Violets and heart entangle
with God. The blessed braces,
overlaps lilies and laurel.

The wreath negotiates shallows and backward
surges, rises and falls, collapses
around logs, loops ferns, changes shape.
Occasionally it hesitates, circles itself
slowly in an eddy: God is any heart
seeing purity. The heart is a blessed
ring of blossoms containing God's vision.

If only the athlete dying young
had been given such a prize.
If only Ophelia had worn
such a wreath. If only Judas
had read this garland.

Still, at any point you might
reach down yourself, catch that ring
of blossoms, lift it up, wear
its beauty and blooming distinction
across your forehead. Look into a mirror.
See what you can see.

In the beginning the silverspot fritillary
comes from the sky. Its mother, in flight,
is only known to it as time, the instant
of that great releasing.

It drifts downward then, a floating dot of egg
more powerful than a single point of star stationary
in an empty night. For a moment it is a grain of ghost
around which the earth circles its heavy forests below.

And when it first emerges from winter with wings,
it rests on a tree inside the slow breathing
of those appendages damp with the sweet oil
of transformation.

Fully itself, the silverspot fritillary is a leaf
that can lift from the branch trembling
like a skeleton of light rising from its own bones.
Over the summer garden its body hovers without body, thin
as a tatter of evening veined by purple sun.

Falling finally in the autumn dark, it tumbles
across the forest floor with the wind, blown
like the dead wings of a grey leaf, like a tatter
of empty star burned by frost.

The creation of the reality existing on this page
could possess the ghost of a salvation, a ghost rising
into everlasting fact by its own skeleton of light, claiming,
as it does now, the purity of time for a holy mother,
a god boundless as sky for a father.

Given like a savior broken
into many sharp, shining pieces
coming like rain to flat cactus
creekbeds, like a savior penetrating
the body like fresh storms of stars,
like showers of fiery, silver sperm,
a bountiful blue savior flitting
like a savior with four double wings
of sun, and a dark savior appearing
where the depth of the lake loses
its visibility, a fat, grinning
savior afloat like a sinking moon,
a savior bound like a sleeping cat
curled up like an egg, multiple
saviors piled like tangled mud frogs
in a spring pond wallow, coming
like a naked savior, like a false
savior walking through himself
as if he were evening smoke rising
through smoke, a miming savior,
a repeating savior like daylight
and daylight like a savior praying
for all and any saviors of saviors.

Because they resurrect too, you know—
a first sharp quiver of mud-buried spine
under sinking ice, quickened frog pulse
skinging like a bead of early redbud still
in the branch, like a beginning spear
of narcissus rising toward the sun
from the rags of its bulb.

Rotund, even shaped a little like Easter
eggs, frogs can be colorful, as if dyed
deliberately by children for basket
arrangements—jungle-orange, hyacinth-red,
splotched, yellow-bellied. And frogs have eggs
themselves, strings and strings of them,
more than is needed, hidden among the roots
and tangles of river reeds, as Baby Moses
once was, shining eggs, like special prizes
necklaced through cress and lotus, glistening
underwater, transparent bauble wombs
holding the beating black dots of limbless,
heart-and-head tadpole embryos.

And frogs sing resurrection sounds,
plinking together, tinging like the wire-hair
notes of many celestial lap-harps
and mandolins, or rumbling and bassing
just like sun-seeking chords of stems
and blades wrenching and forging the way
underground in their power push upward.

Like the reaffirming spring abundances
of violets, lilies, madders, starworts
and rosettes of sundew, frogs ascend anew
through anointing wet and warmth, mill

and move in the wash of light upon April
creekbeds and ponds.

Here comes one now. See first her bronze
iridescent eyes just resting on the water's
shimmering plain. She floats to full view,
click and glide. She's ripple flying,
wingborne, emerging now into the blackroot
rushes of the bank, a living body entire,
clearing, rising up once again out of the dead
winter earth, reborn.

Surely, for frogs,
isn't this enough to qualify?

He roars in red. So I pluck him, pinch
him off right at the flat green star
of his fiercest electricity.

I sponge him all over, gently,
with my thumb, under a spigot
of running water.

He lets me soothe him with cream, tap and roll
him once in sweet powders. He lets me put my lips
around his pudgy tip, bite and pull, suck,
break. O the sugar and sap in my mouth then,
the searing blossom-juices spilling (a napkin
is required at the corners) the constant ping
of tiny firecrackers in my teeth!

I destroy his effort and sweat. I shiver, swallowing
all of his sizzle. I exude his peculiar fragrance.
He becomes my momentary flush and swell,
the same faint draw, the very blush
of my ear napes and nipples.

All evening long we engage
in our religion. I am his servant. I behold
and dissolve him. I coo at his company.
I hum and he vibrates. He allows me,
lavishes me, generously bestows upon me
that which he alone, as god may bestow:
the power to proclaim
with a faith so perfect it disappears,
strawberry.

Here before the bur oak was born,
creating the space its place became,
and after the bur oak died,
taking back the oblivion
it had invented,

                present before the past
of Sheng-mo's frog on its throne
of lotus leaf began and after
the future of Sheng-mo's studious
frog on its paper leaf ceased,

                         after
and before sunlight yesterday reached
the bottom of the unknown spring
where no one watched, where perhaps
albino fish and pale water spiders
swam without morning praise
or amen,

           existent in the silence before
the wind's rumbling and scraping
and moaning sounded through the fearsome
spaces between the desert stars

                      and present
in the silence following the death
of wind and the demise of desert,

                    here
long before the woolly arctic rhinoceros
and long after,

              and before the herd
of fleeing prehistoric horses
and following the herd of fleeing
prehistoric horses and before
the night before hands transformed

the blind cave wall to the stone-thunder
and eyes of those horses in flight
and before stone and during
                              and after
eyes and hands and before and after:
                                    this is about
whatever is that is what I have here posited to be
throughout

FIVE

For Emma and Edith

They sit, side by side on the bed, sewing
the buttons back on her dress. Each needle
slides through each button as easily as a hair
of metal light, through the floral cotton print,
pulling the threads behind, drawing the round
disks tight.

After he grabbed her by her housedress, breaking
the buttons all the way down the front, he tore
the new yellow curtains from the kitchen windows,
left by the back, kicking the screen door, wrenching
it so the spring bent backward.

Side by side, shoulders touching, the dress
spread over their knees, they sit together
on the bed, gold in the summer dusk, threading,
knotting.

The curtains, yellow, rickrack-trimmed, torn
from their windows, lay on the linoleum; her dress
hung open, hose slipping, buttons scattered
on the floor, the screen door shuddering.

Side by side in the rainforest, surrounded by wild
ginger and beadlily, a nurse log rich with licorice
ferns and draperies of club moss hanging
in the maples overhead, they sit together
in the day darkness, looping thread with needles
like splinters of light, their fingers unburnt
by the brilliance.

He grabbed the neck of her dress, tearing
down and apart, one button striking her cheek.
The screen door cracked open with a sharp

shot, the spring screaming backward, the curtains
collapsed on the linoleum floor.

Beside the ocean, a Greek-blue sea, they sew,
shoulders touching, the dress spread between them
on their knees, its cotton flowers like wings
fluttering against the white sky. And in the winter
garden, snow caught in each violet crease
of sinewy vine, each cross of the lattice, they sit
beneath the arbor, their needles glinting
like icicles of fire. And in the field, in place,
they bend their heads together, their fingers
looping, fastening, as the foxtail grasses fall, loop,
fasten, rise, the threads knotted, secured.

Sitting on the chenille spread, side by side,
Moberly, Missouri, 1949, they work together alone
before the open window, whispering; the evening star,
upon which, they fully realize, they have no need to wish,
is just beginning to show.

One might arrive on a balmy day, a calm surf
of sky overhead, the clouds enfolding themselves
as if there were no one else but themselves to love,
sinking and surfacing, embracing their own pale
grey hue like the grey under-down of a snowy owl,
their blue like the fade of violet in a glacial
crevasse, the white sky of a grey sun so far away.
A prayer I fully recognize.

Another prayer might appear as the glistening
edge of a green tendril curled around the thin
wire of its fence, holding on with a purity of focus
and intention that validates the universe;
another during the blind of a moonless night,
the way every star, without breath, breathes
light. Is receiving a prayer a reply?

Once a promise came as the taste of butter
on fresh corn shucked and grilled, once
as the fragrance of white gardenia tied with white
ribbon, once a silent pleading prayer, loud
in its ferocity, when I saw a man stomp a small
snake, its open mouth helpless against his boot.
From whence come such messages?

Yesterday, again, within a snow-filled forest
of pine, every hard ice-covered spear of life and I
alert, motionless, listening . . . one scarce slip
of snow, resounding.

Most lie low, flourishing with damp,
harvesting sunlight, no commotion, mosses
mouse-silent even through wind and hail,
stoic through motors roaring fumes,
through fat-clawed bears grubbing.

They can soothe the knife-edges of stones
with frothy leaf by leaf of grey/green life,
and burned-ground mosses cover destruction,
charred stumps, trees felled and blackened.
Cosmopolitan mosses likewise salve
sidewalk cracks, crumbling walls.

They root in thin alpine air, on sedentary
sand dunes, cling to cliff seeps beneath
spilling springs. For rest, they make mats
on streamside banks, for pleasure produce silky
tufts, wavy brooms of themselves in woodlands
for beauty, red roof moss for whim, elf
cap, haircap, sphagnum for nurturing.

No fossil record of note, no bone
history, so lenient they possess only
those memories remembered.

I believe they could comfort the world
with their ministries. That is my hope,
even though this world be a jagged rock,
even though this rock be an icy berg of blue
or a mirage of summer misunderstood
(moss balm for misunderstanding),
even though this world be blind and awry
and adrift, scattering souls like spores
through the deep of a starlit sea.

Present early, the drawing in, the sucking
and swallowing, beginning in the infant floating
in the womb, the lips pursing and releasing,
a vestigial thumb at the mouth.

When oranges were rare (and even now)
people preferred to cut a rind circle from the top,
press the whole fruit to their lips, close
their eyes and suckle, swallowing the promise,
taking in the consoling act of taking in.

Isn't the suckling, swallowing closure felt
far in the back of the throat between breaths
the same mesmerizing motion an ebbing tide uses
to suck itself back out of tidal pools and beaches,
back into the merge of an all-consuming sea?

And there is a sucking that holds hard
to its source. All prairie grasses, taiga forests,
sedum and wild roots grasp and draw water
from the earth, and also a sucking that holds on
for sustenance, the remora to its shark, the longnose
sucker fish swooping algae from river bottom
rocks and mud. One can almost hear the suck
of every slide a snail takes, the tight pull
of a gecko's feet up a slick stone wall.

The gravity of a black hole vortex sucks in
even light. If light is synonymous with perception,
then, while swallowing light, what kind of peace
is it that a black hole possesses?

The soothing lull begins, the suckling lull
surpassing even the lull of the body gently rocking,
by cradle, by chair, a lull even more enduring

than the lull of the body slowly swaying
round and round with the turning sky.

Sometimes, when sucking a leaf of mint,
a twig of cinnamon, or drawing water
through a straw, or taking in the sweet
of honeysuckle, the nipple in the mouth,
the milk . . . a peace, succulent and pure,
becomes the soul, older than sleep, older
than earth, older than the gods.

Hasn't the river poplar learned so well to mold itself
to that blowing branch-shaped vacancy existing
inside a flickering summer by the bank?
And hasn't the moon copied perfectly the lake's dark
dream of possessing a circular stone of brilliance
in each and every wave?

The bud of the fire pink has obviously shaped itself
without error or deviation to a coming pleasure
in red, and the peeper, climbing the leather leaf
beside the pond, has arranged itself to fit precisely
the pearlescent sound of spring's origination.

Charity and creation, like gloves, must always
have had five finger-shells apiece into which the soul
could form the flesh and bones of its double dexterity.

A small white egret alone, gliding at eye-level
over the mown field, long neck curved inward, legs
held straight back and pressed along its body,
has so perfectly imitated the sailing bone and wing
of grace, the bold gut and motivation of redemption,
that someone watching today might be tempted
to say and believe: the only name it ever had
was savior.

1.

Sands, in wild winds of surging waves
over the desert dunes, sing with the tones
of tiny pebbles moving all together, a shifting
of dust grains humming and moaning
over the growing and diminishing dunes.

2.

His body in the mirror is the color
of sands. The song he sings is the voice
of light shining like waves of wind
passing over his body inside the glass.

3.

The mirror sings with the color of sand
in the highest octaves of light.

4.

Have you ever listened to sands sing
with gold light as they fall in threads
through the needle-eye opening
at the center of an hour-glass globe?

Why not arrange such globes in rows
before a window of sun, each globe
a different width, a different height
of refined or rudimentary glass, clear
amber rose, a tinted blue of noon sky,
and listen to the chorus?

And then why not turn the globes
upside down and over again to hear
sands sing one more time?

5.

The desert dunes are singing, wind-risen
voices from a primeval earth, haunting,
pacific, pining and irate. We listen
for the repeating message we remember.
Their songs are only tumbling pebble grains;
their words are only notes of swirling dust,
sings the eternal light, Emanuel.

I'm not certain what the center is,
but it's easy to find in most flowers,
bringing the tip of the finger to bear
on the yellow disk of the oxeye daisy
or the black bump of the prairie coneflower
around which its radiating petals spur.
And anyone's vision is led easily to the center
of the painted trillium, the coordinate
where all scarlet-blue threads descend
and come together as one.

The orange and black banded argiope
marks the center of her hoop by the zigzag
crochet of her silk, by her own eight-clawed
crouching on that knotted stitch. And the center
of the circus ring is the invisible notion
the jingling scarlet-feathered,
grey-flecked ponies prance around.

I once heard a dancer say the center
fluctuated as she moved, her ear tilted
upward being the center, then her elbow
akimbo, then her foot lifted and held, the place
where her spirit temporarily resided.

Though I don't have an adequate definition,
I think the center is what the mountain sheep's
horn knows to orbit, something the eye
of the short-eared owl knows not to release.
It's the non-existent point that tiny ice spears
in snow crystals find and make actual.

And I suppose the most secure center
is the spot where the tether is attached,
the looped metal stake the mongrel pulls

against constantly, tracking predictable
circle paths around it in the grass, the stake
that prevents a floating, tumbling, masterless
vertigo, that allows an aspiration
to be established even in the blindness
of midnight.

It seems time doesn't have a center,
only edges over which one falls
year after year. Though if it did
and we found it, we could tether to it,
circle that center savior like show ponies
in a ring or fight it like wild wolves
on chains creating raucous intentions
or simply move inward, touch it, crouch
there and cling, making patterns like crystals,
making homes like gods.

SIX

Seven Variations on Redefinition

I. ACCOMMODATION

In this field of buttercups, cream cups,
curly dock and winged dock, blooming,
blooming, honey bees, silvery blues,
primrose, showy thistle, and yellow
clover, too many flowers, overmuch
floribunda—there is no space, no room
for pronouncing *meager* or *miserly*,
no cell of silence for *restraint* to inhabit.

Among the rocks and rubble bottoms
of the tidal line, an eight legged, two pincered,
single toothed, globular, pear shaped,
totally vacant emptiness exists, present
and waiting for the spiny spider crab
to become and occupy it.

So surrounded by thunders crashing
like boulders in avalanches splitting
and shattering against each other,
so stunned by the sporadic, inner-breast
shock of rain explosions, lightning whipping
again and again—she can imagine no sphere
in which to imagine a murmuring lullaby.

Although he had eyes, he could never
see the stars because his heart
had no place for them.

This horizontal angle of evening
sunlight, the calm slant of shadow
on the walk, that jay's stark cry
repeated, and the spicy scent of autumn
inherent to the stalwart leaves, these,
together with mouth, hunger, and hand,
accommodate perfectly—an apple.

I don't know how the wood thrush knows
how to match the pitch and fall of its cry
exactly to the pitch and fall the mountain ridge
makes against the evening sky.

And I don't know how the purple beebalm
knows how to pattern the spray and spread
of its spear-pointed blossoms exactly to the thrust
and parry, the petal-thin whirr and circling
thrimble of the hunting hummingbird.

Each round lobe of the three-leafed clover
fits itself perfectly into each green note
of the tree frog's treble, and each tree frog
swells its tremolo in cylindrical bunches
of three-toned rings.

The warblers, all together, place their calls
as leaf upon leaf of forest overlay
and shadow. And see how the black branches
of the spruce against the grey sky
have shaped themselves in their ascent
to the same spikes and needles
the black dog yelps
from his chain beside the shed.

What is it that I imitate? to what structure
do I meld? my stance, my cry and mumble
fitting exactly into the chinks
and snugness of some *other*? What is it
that makes its own body, that finds the steps
of its own motion against the outline
of my voice?

There must be something. There must.
Since my conviction may be its very stature
and its very spine, how can I be convinced otherwise?

The Frost Place
Summer 1987

The slow, mellow poplar drifting at dusk,
holding in its shadows the invisible bodies
of two great horned spirits, is the reason
for the low cello tones of their calls branching out
one to the other through the silent *ah* of evening.

The fiery red and green reason
is the holly berry bush against snow.

To fill the forest with two eyes of black
sun and copper fur flashing by in flight
is the fox racing reason.

The sun sound of water pellets
dropping separately, simultaneously,
in strings of light from the snow-covered
eaves is the falling reason for melting.

The cry she hears, coming from beyond
the stone wall and wooden gate toward which
she walks, is the reason she stops, looks back
at the way she came and no longer knows it.

The reason for the fluttering white silk
on the waves tonight is the moon rabbit
taking a dip, floating and swimming,
shape-shifting like laughter finally
free against the serious sea.

All action, it leaps, faster than the eye
can follow, from treetip to trestle tower,
from cedar roof to harvested fields,
cartwheels and spins, leaps again
and attacks, slithering up dead oaks
and dry junipers, captures, holds
close, strangles, suffocates

in its consumption, becomes all mouth,
gulping and swallowing entire acres
of sere and withered stalks, the curled
leaves and remnant grasses of autumn,
of drought, gasps, sinks, lifts, continues

dances like no other, soars, swooping
with its many wings, scatters ragged
flames and sparks of confetti in its wake
through the sky, invents sex with the wind
as they fly sun-bound together

bombastic, a spontaneous explosion
in dusty silos of hot sizzling grains

whose Creator is lightning, whose
Giving God is air

hovers, quiet and low on sparse
clearings as if the earth were the best
of keepers, forms brilliant rings
of red-orange, floors of black inside
these circles where ghosts of gremlins
cavort, swaying like smoke

skittish at the lake's edge, angry
at rivers, averse to frost, hibernates

in flint, lies still among crumpled
papers and oily rags, rises up, a rowdy
resurrection with the first flick

buries itself in warm ashes and coals,
sleeps with one eye open.

Black endures, like thornapple, like coyote, like ebony
locust and ironclad beetle, like the most engrossing
nether level of a packrat midden.

Even single and scattered, *black is indivisible
and everywhere*, consuming everything with delicacy,
as if believing (within this singularity) that the numeral
one is forever plural. Thus *black is always present*
and on time when summoned for black tea
with the Forgotten Queen of Black in her tomb.

Black, as demonstrated here, *slits and slices* the day,
parceling it in the way spears of oak leaves above parcel
the forest floor into sharp shadows, which shadows
are cousins to black. *Black is both many and solo*
in congregational callings, cawing conversations
with serrated edges of sound sawing across harvests
and thoroughfares, through myth and notion.

Someone might think those *silhouettes of black*,
flocking like crows, like broken pieces of thunder clouds,
like sodden leaves rising into the sky, are *the most accurate
of thoughts replicating structures of philosophy gleaned
from the black bible of sleep.*

When *black gathers* along highways on winter nights,
*becoming a cadre of soldier-statues marching as crosses
in single file*, icy snow like remnants of fallen stars covering
their shoulders, then even the blind can't see them.
Black is that close.

Like the thought of a silver ring lying locked inside
a silver box, like the idea of zero on a moonless night,
ultimately *black fills the circle of whatever is missing.*

As mentioned before, *black is indivisible, a negative*
in itself like the hue that it is, like faith deeper
than your heart's need for it, deeper than the black
pupil of your eye enlarging now to merge with black.

But don't ever believe you can join black's cabal,
no matter how you might wish it. *Black is better*
than your words. Black is beyond your prayers.

They are not porcelain painted in hues of autumn
chestnut, brisk brown or white with splots of black,
but when they are painted porcelain arranged,
alert, and facing toward the horizon beyond
the mantelpiece, they announce themselves.

They are not crystal, but when they are crystal,
the sun flows through their brilliantly empty bodies
all day. They are orange fire at evening, blue fog
filled with the moon at midnight.

When they are blue fog, they leave their rigid
bodies, envelope the shore, become gentler,
more malleable than the thin bendable grasses
and sighs of the dunes where they float.

If dropped and broken, they are pieces
of fallen glass stars on the floor.

When they are blood and bones and loved,
they sleep and dream and are human.

Harold is top dog, Canis Major, of the pack.
Squire is his sidekick.

When they have wings, they are bird dogs.
When they are bird dogs and fly in the heavens,
they are angels hunting the night with Orion.

When they are shepherds of sheep watching
over their dozing flocks on the hillsides, they see

themselves winging the night with Orion.
They howl for the peace of themselves on earth.

When they rise and set during August nights
they are called the dog days of summer.

Those who aren't dogs call them hounds,
call them mongrels and pooches and curs and cock
fighters and bitches and studs, ratters, flea bags.

They scratch at the dust and pretend to have horns
when they are called bull dogs.

Harold is Alpha dog, sire of Jack and Knave.
Squire is his deputy, Canis Minor. LoLo
is his consort. God has ordained it.

When God loosens their leashes and lets them go,
they race through the underbrush of the forest,
digging among fecund leaves, rooting out voles
and newts. They romp the meadow, cavort
in the river, lap and shake its crazy flowing froth.
They roll in fertile feces and maggoty carcasses.
This is their ritual of worship.

Afterward, like the earth-covered dogs they are,
like the holy dogs they are, like the anointed
pilgrims they are, each one always comes back
to the word, to the whistle, to the touch of the hand.
Each always comes home, like Lassie.

We don't mind our eyes being painted open
in perpetual surprise on the sides
of our stuffed heads. We don't mind
the permanent bit and bridle sewn and stapled
to our faces. And we don't mind the hard,
bare broom-handles which are our only withers
and our only hooves and our only spines,
which contain the carvings and constrictions
of our only hearts.

For, on the days when we are taken up
and lifted, we are transported far
beyond these walls and ordinary rock fences,
carried as if flying across the earth, over
ravines and rock-filled streams, through populations
of fleeing ricebirds and lacewings, into steep caves
of honeysuckle and along the spider-crossed
pathways of many unmapped forests.

And when we are ridden boldly and certainly
down the open hillsides, racing into the afternoon
as if into battle, our rag manes blowing,
we know we become at once all the thundering
convictions of that daring run. And when we rear
and scream during the rush of such moments,
we can hear in our voices the words
of voices which are not our own.

We are given this additional gift: Galloping
beside the still lake on a clear autumn day,
we may look at its surface and see,
astride our sticks, the presence, the hands

and breath and gesture, the freedom
and the beauty of our own souls.

We don't mind it, then,
when we are left again lying alone
by the garden gate, one eye on earth,
one eye on heaven, our cotton brains
drinking equally the dew of grasses, the dew
of stars; for we know we can define
the extraordinary, and we can distinguish
the holy, and we can recognize ourselves
further beyond ourselves
than any other of god's creatures.

SEVEN

The moment when the sky turned to one solid
plate of grey beginning its dull spread
from no definable point at all;

when every thrasher and bank swallow
and kite who called
called from faraway, out of earshot,

behind the flat predictable hills of common grey;
when every insect that rose
rose motionless above the lake and became an invisible

silent-grey against the plate-grey sky;
when the rough-bark back of the toads sank
with no effort, out of sight

into the rough-bark beds of mud slowly smoothing themselves
to an indifferent sky-pale sheen
and the lines of the spider lilies bent backward

into themselves blending perfectly with the boundaries
of the floating hearts moving in and out
of their own vacillating facts;

and the name of the blue teal's cry merged
without detection into the name
of the dissipating odor of the butterfly pea;

when the breezes stood stockstill
over the empty, unnoticeably quiet
waters of grey,

that was the same moment
when the pen rolled into the infinity
just beyond the fingertips,

when the poet lay back among the disappearing grasses,
closed her eyes beneath the vanishing heavens
and slept.

I was convinced I had an opened wing
and could fly, but it was only because the space
between my outstretched arm and rib cage
was filled by the motion of the red-tailed hawk
gliding beside me till dawn.

I was certain I had hoary fangs and a honey-covered
tongue, but it was only the hairy mask, the wide
woofing face that came down to cover my own
when I closed my eyes.

I thought my navel, my nipples, the stratums
of my body below, were blooming buds, knots of petals,
but it was only because the rising moon, disking
and plowing, colored them violet, softened and opened
them carefully layer by layer, creating a garden.

I sank and rose easily and rapidly in the sea,
it seemed, on my stomach, on my back, pumping
and pedaling, parting forests of filefish
and lanternfish, lifting with the four-winged
flying fish, but it was merely the suckered
points of that deep surf carrying me,
tossing me, turning me round and round
on its multiple tentacles.

I thought I yipped and I thought I yowled
and I thought I preened and pecked, digging up,
swallowing slick tubers and pods. I thought I curled
sinuously up and down my own stem, drew in,
tucked my eyes beneath the helmet over my head.

I was certain I agreed, separated, spread,
multiplied, pushed up and overturned by myself
thousands of pebbles and stones, even boulders,
even stars in the field.

I believed all of this and I knew
I was good. But it was just the winding
ribbon, the silk sky-wrapping, Möbius strip,
the swaddling, and the breast all night long
wherever I put my mouth.

Tonight I want to be somewhere still
and safe, dark and anonymous, some place composed,
not of particles, the kind that ignite and extinguish,
lock and release, leap without purpose, leap
without leaping, orbit to orbit. I'm tired
of excitement like that;

tonight I want a place reconciled and indivisible,
composed just of the whole of itself—inside the unblemished
wooden shell of a sweet pecan, for instance, where the seal
is complete and perfect, no seam of evening,
no seepage of day;

or within the very last knot of the conch's wound
coral circles where the hold is firm and certain
(anything winding that far and deep to find me
would cease to be itself long before it arrived);

or inside a clay jug made with no opening, one formed
around me and closed on the potter's wheel
then decorated with blossom-shapes of written
blessings, a magic against pieces, a magic against parts.

Tonight I want to be enclosed by a soft warm
purse drawn tightly shut, like that space safe
inside a snow-buried she-bear where two furless
cubs lie, scarlet and white, curled around one another,
living, unborn and blind.

To go in, to go into a place like that,
leaving outside even my wish to go in . . .
such a pleasure could only be invented and so desired
by one who knows nothing of silence, nothing of stasis,
only the wafting, waning shrill of the absolute.

Not as a white-winged hawk releases
and falls sinking on the wind until its wings
swerve upward riding the current again
toward the sun; not as the flower-covered
barrette is unlatched and her hair, fully
freed, falls across her shoulders in a flight
of its own invention;

and not the freefall that comes before
the parachute spreads and opens above
like a prayer and halts the plunge;
and not the tumbling fall of an acrobat
before he catches the trapeze his partner
drops as she falls to catch his feet,
not any of those falls;

not the continual plummeting fall
of mountain snowmelt creating icy weather
in summer; nor the spider gliding down
her string, floating more than falling
in descent just as day falls and drifts
in its own ways into night; and not as one falls
with eyes closed into sleep where faith
is with the falling; nor as one falls
into love where riotous ascent begins
simultaneous with the falling.

But consider the falling that is immutable:
the naked body of a nestling lying spilled
and broken on the sidewalk; wind-felled fruit,
sick odor of rotting pulp below the tree, slick
mass oozing into earth; the cold frightening
stillness of those who lie fallen in battle.

And remember the story of the bleakest fall,
the fall of those who once were angels,
who fell and fell into the deepest chasm
of blindness, irredeemable, never to rise,
never to hope to rise. Pity their god.

From *The Journals of a Lost Believer*

It's an obsession now, this matching
and measuring, comparing, for instance,
the coral-violet of the inner lip
of a queen conch to the last rim of dusk
on the purple-flowering raspberry
to the pure indigo of the bird-voiced
tree frog's twittering tongue, then converting
the result to an accepted standard
of rose-scarlet gradations.

It's difficult to say which is greater—
the brevity of the elk's frosty bellow
or the moments of fog sun-lifted
through fragrances of blue spruce
or the fading flavor in one spoonful
of warm chocolate rum.

I mark out space by ten peas
strung on a string. The pane perimeter
of my window, for instance, is twenty-eight
lengths up, twelve lengths over.
Seventy pea-strings stretch from bed
to door. Four go round my neck.

My longing for you is more painful
than the six-times folding, doubling
and doubling, of a coyote's
most piercing cry, more inconsolable
than a whole night of moonlight blinded
by thunderclouds, more constant
than black at the center of a cavern
stone below leagues of granite.

I gauge my cold by the depth
of stillness in the pod-heart of a frozen
wren. I time my breath by the faltering
leaves of aspen in wind. I count the circles
of my dizziness by the spreading rings
of rain-lassos on the pond, by the repeating
bell chimes of the corridor clock,
by the one unending ring of the horizon.

Where is the tablet, where the rule, where
the steel weights, the balance, the book,
properly to make measure of a loss
so grand and deep I can spread and stitch it
to every visible star I name—Arcturus,
Spica, Vega, Regulus—in this dark
surrounding dark surrounding dark?

For all those in need

Whether they bend as compliantly as black leaves
curved and hanging in heavy dew in the grey dawn,
or whether they wait as motionless as ice-coated
insects and spears of roots on a northern cliff;

whether they tighten once like the last white edge
of primrose taken suddenly skyward
by a gust of frost, or swallow as hard as stones
careened and scattered by a current of river;

whether they mourn by the bright line of grief
running like a spine of glass straight through the sound
of their songs, or whether they fall quietly
through indefinite darkness like a seed of sorrel
bound alive beneath snow;

whether their eyes are wet in the night, their foreheads
damp and fragrant, or whether the orifices of their bodies
are as dry and withered as broken cholla
lying on a dusty plain;

whether they mourn in multitudes, blessed
like a congregation of winter forests moaning for the white
drifting children of storms they can never remember,
or whether they grieve separately, divided
even from themselves, parted like golden plovers blown
and calling over a buffeted sea;

something must come to them, something as clear and fair
and continuous as the eye of the bluegill open in calm water,
something as silent as the essential spaces of breath
heard inside the voice naming all of their wishes,

something touching them in the same way the sun deep
in the pit of the pear touches the spring sky by the light
of its own leaf. A comfort understood like that
must be present now and possible.

EIGHT

They know how to hide, passing easily in and out
of existence with light among the swaying
stalks of marsh mallow. They have taught
the shadows of the wood pine to flicker with tail
and sun-blotched plumage. They know how to disappear
in the crack between hillside and heaven while the eye
is still watching the wing of itself.

Without effort they can become ferned and ruffled
rocks lying in the fields, or rufous rumps
of prairie rose, or waves of night sweeping
through the current of the treetops.

Or they can appear outright, scarlet
on a snowy field, glistening black in a bare
white sycamore, a grey rush of down swooping
ten feet from the face, only to be called at such times
hallucination. And when their taut bodies are clearly
witnessed, tipped and buffeted like wired cloth
in the wind above the ocean cliffs, they are simply named
vulnerability. And if they are seen again soaring
and diving without motion over the summer plains,
they are labeled ecstasy.

They sail, silver and gold under the sea,
just as if their wings were gelatinous stubs, and ascend,
making feathers of their scales, rising out of the water,
mistaken then for angels in their white salt gowns.
On some evenings they fill the sky completely, squeezing
the vision, blocking out the dusk, leaving no space
against which they might be distinguished.
The description of their passing then is attributed
to fantasy. They come as calling flocks over tinted lakes
confident they will never be seen as themselves.

And they know exactly how to sing all night, beak
in the ear, making the brain their territory,
just to be called at dawn a dream.

Watch how they can fly openly, fleeced with brown,
streaked with russet and dun, a maze of turquoise
and green, coming so close to the eye
that a single feather causes total blindness,
as they demonstrate once again their only reality
for all those who pursue a study of elusion.

The phylum Porifera (organ-pipe
sponge, nipple sponge, red beard
sponges, slime sponge) might be said
to compose a sacred litany.
Some equations (Pythagorean,
Schrödinger's) are called sublime.
And the periodic table of atomic
weights, the listed twenty-two
bones of the skull seem to me to be
recitations of devotion.

Whose configuration, whose manner
is it that we find in the studied spring
and rat-tailed gallop of a sperm released,
or in the recorded roll of a budding
trout lily, in the ordered relay
of a network of neurons discovering
the chin barbel, luminous lure
of a dark sea fish?

How could the mapping of Neptune's
arc of moonlets or the observation
of spindles in a grasshopper cell
ever be corrupt?

Lycosa gulosa, the forest wolf spider,
found by its silver eyes in woody litter
and given a word of its own for the first
time, takes on the radiance of its name.
Then the mockingbirds of *Mimidae*,
the titmice of *Paridae*, the woodpeckers

of *Picidae* must comprise at once
a remarkable pronouncement of light.

Don't these discovered and enunciated details
all together form a structure themselves,
a storied edifice possessing patterns
of seeing, a presence, a spirit?

Enter here as well.

Having watched him walking away
from the beginning, they know,
as they know a silhouette of cypress
in a marsh wind or the motion
of brown river water under ice,
the set of his shoulders, the gesture
of his stride. Once so near
that every pearl button, every warp
and weft of his apparel could be studied,
he has proceeded daily, his back
turned, to move away, farther
and farther from them, solitary
across the same long field.

He was there for years,
every morning the first thing
they saw, as statuesque as the cold
dawn sun passing through flocking
ricebirds, stirring the spiders
in the bittersweet. Often, sitting
on the lawn in the evenings,
they would catch sight of him again,
moving with the same methodical grace
through a maze of fireflies
toward the tightening and knotting
of the new night. Waking later,
peering out their windows at the moon,
they could always discern his receding
figure by the steadiness of his shadow
among the skittery shadows of the clouds
disintegrating over the blowing grasses.

He continues his departure now
through the plush and aromatic foams
of each spring, through the cracking

currents and frozen swells of succeeding
winters, becoming smaller and smaller
as they watch, a broken twig
on the landscape, no bigger
than a pod of sumac, a sparrow print
against the snow, hardly visible,
even though they peruse
the distance with their eyes
strained and shaded.

And don't they know him completely,
don't they finally perceive
him fully and most perfectly
during that moment when,
from the far fragmentary
blue sketch of rain on the horizon,
from the desolate, barely
disturbed line of the plain,
from the immeasurably minute
figure of focus remaining
in their eyes, he sinks away
and disappears?

Of the unhindered motion in the million
swirled and twisted grooves of the juniper
driftwood lying in the sand; taking leave
of each sapphire and amber thread
and each iridescent bead of the swallowtail's
wing and of the quick and clever needle
of the seamstress in the dark cocoon
that accomplished the stitching.

Goodbye to the long pale hairs
of the swaying grass flowers, so like, in grace
the color and bearing, the nodding
antennae of the green valley grasshopper
clinging to its blade; and to the staircase
shell of the butter-colored wentletrap
and to the branches of the sourwood
making their own staircase with each step
upward they take and to the spiraling
of the cobweb weaver twirling
as it descends on its silk
out of the shadows of the pitch pine.

Taking leave of the sea
of spring, that grey-green swell
slowly rising, spreading, its heavy
wisteria-scented surf filled
with darting, gliding, whistling
fish, a current of cries, an undertow
of moans and buzzes, so pervasive
and penetrating and alluring
that the lungs adapt
to the density.

Determined not to slight the knotted
rockweed or the beach plum or the white
blue-tipped petals of the five spot;
determined not to overlook the pursed
orange mouth of each maple leaf
just appearing or the entire chorus
of those open leaves in full summer forte.

My whole life, a parting
from the brazen coyote thistle and the reticent,
tooth-ridged toad crab and the proud,
preposterous sage grouse.

And you mustn't believe that the cessation
which occurs here now is more
than illusory. The ritual
of this leave-taking continues
beyond these lines, in a whisper
beside the window, below my breath
by the river, without noise
through the clearing at midnight,
even in the dark, even in sleep
continues, out-of-notice,
private, incessant.

I think it's a multiplication of sight,
like after a low hovering autumn rain
when the invisible webs of funnel weavers
and sheetweb weavers all at once are seen
where they always were, spread and looping
the grasses, every strand, waft and leaf-
crest elucidated with water-light and frost,
completing the fullest aspect of *field*.

Or maybe the grace of death is split-second
transformation of knowledge, an intricate,
turning realization, as when a single
sperm-embracing deer ovum transforms,
in an instant, from stasis to replicating,
star-shifting shimmer, rolls, reaches,
alters its plane of intention, becomes
a hoofing, thumping host of purpose.

I can imagine not merely
the falling away of blank walls
and blinds in that moment, not merely
a shutter flung open for the first time
above a valley of interlocking forests
and constellations but a sweeping,
penetrating circumference of vision
encompassing both knotweed bud
and its seed simultaneously, seeing
blood bone and its ash as one,
the repeated light and fall and flight
of hawk-owl and tundra vole
as a union of origin and finality.

A mathematics of flesh and space might
take hold if we ask for it in that last
moment, might appear as if it had always

existed within the eyes, translucent,
jewel-like in stained glass patterns
of globes and measures, equations
made evident by a revelation of galaxies
in the knees, spine, fingers, all
the ceasings, all the deaths within deaths
that compose the body becoming at once
their own symbolic perception and praise
of river salt, blooms and breaths, strings,
strains, sun-seas of gravels and gills;
this one expression breaking, this same
expression healing.

NOTES

The poems collected in *Quickening Fields* were written during the years 1980–2016. None of these poems have appeared previously in any of my books. All of the poems, with the exception of six, were published previously in the various journals listed in the Acknowledgments.

Kioka ("The Thing in Itself") is a fictional character, a cosmopolitan seer and next of kin to all wildlife and lands of the earth. He appears in several of my books and is especially featured in *Legendary Performance*.

ACKNOWLEDGMENTS

I am very grateful to the editors of the journals where the poems in this book first appeared. I appreciate their encouragement and thank them for their support of my work and the work of many other contemporary poets.

Thanks to Dom Zuccone, Leslie Ullman, Derek Sheffield, and Dennis Held for their friendship and conversations, to Simmons Buntin for his e-mail that instigated the beginning of this book, to Stephen Corey for his encouragement over many years and his editorial assistance with my recent essay (appearing in *The Georgia Review*) addressing the background of *Quickening Fields*.

As always, thanks to Paul Slovak for his thoughtful attention to my work and his steady hand shepherding the manuscript through early drafts to published book.

And to John, my husband, with me and for me in every way throughout from the beginning, my love, my history, my home, forever thankful.

Cream City Review: "Playroom: The Visionaries"
Domestic Crude: "Waking God at Dawn"
Fine Madness: "The Woodland Snail at Twilight"; "Capturing a
    Wild Pony"
The Georgia Review: "Particular Falls"; "The Congregating of Stars";
    "Noonday and a Deep Idea of Yellow"
Great Stream Review: "Is Knowledge of the Universe Holy?"
The Gettysburg Review: "Gospel"
First published by the Catholic Health Association of the United States
    in *Health Progress*: "Receiving Prayers"
Image: "The Moss Method"; "Fire in Freedom"
The Kenyon Review: "Death Vision"

Literature and Belief: "The Estate of Solemnity"; "The Word (Sun After Rain)"

The Massachusetts Review: "Keeping the Body Warm"; "I Thought I Heard a White-Haired Man with a Purple Tie Say, 'The Mind Creates What It Perceives.'"

The Missouri Review: "The Art of Imitation"; "Taking Leave"; "Seeing the God Statement"

Poem-a-Day, Academy of American Poets (www.poets.org/poets.org/poem-day): "Forth into View, Random Warriors"

Poetry: "Finding the Cat in a Spring Field at Midnight"; "The Abandonment"; "Statement Preliminary to the Invention of Solace"; "The Thing in Itself"; "How the Old See Death"; "Calling to Measure"

Poetry Northwest: "Rumors of Snow, Christmas Eve"; "Pursuing the Study of a Particular Reality"; "The Imagination Imagines Itself to Be a God"; "Coming Back"; "The God of Sunday Evening, June 7, 1987"; "Earth-Night Errors"

Prairie Schooner: "Faith and Certainty: Arctic Circles"; "The Older Kid"

River City: "Next to Sleep"; "Grandmother's Sister"

Seattle Review: "Easter Frogs"

South Carolina Review: "Crux"; "Winter Camping"

Terrain.org: "Young Summer Sating"; "Musical and Motoring Cycles"

Terminus: "The Most Primitive Peace"; "The Highest Octaves of Light: A Canticle"; "Accommodation"; "Grand Sky/Grand Prairie"

TriQuarterly: "Predestination"

Pattiann Rogers has published fourteen books of poetry and two collections of essays. Her most recent books are *Holy Heathen Rhapsody* (Penguin, 2013) and *The Grand Array: Writings on Nature, Science, and Spirit* (Trinity University Press, 2010). *Song of the World Becoming: New and Collected Poems 1981–2001* (Milkweed Editions) was a finalist for the *Los Angeles Times* Book Prize and an Editor's Choice in *Booklist. Firekeeper: New and Selected Poems* was a finalist for the Lenore Marshall Award and a *Publishers Weekly* Best Book of 1994. Rogers is the recipient of two NEA Grants, a Guggenheim Fellowship, and a 2005 Literary Award in Poetry from the Lannan Foundation. Her poems have won three prizes from *Poetry*, the Theodore Roethke Prize from *Poetry Northwest*, two Strousse Awards from *Prairie Schooner*, and five Pushcart Prizes. Her work has appeared in *Best American Poetry* in 1996 and 2009, and in *Best Spiritual Writing*, 1999, 2000, 2001, 2002, and 2010. In May, 2000, Rogers was in residence at the Rockefeller Foundation's Bellagio Study and Conference Center in Bellagio, Italy. She has been a visiting writer at numerous universities and colleges and was associate professor at the University of Arkansas from 1993 to 1997. Rogers's papers are archived in the Sowell Family Collection of Literature, Community, and the Natural World at Texas Tech University. She is the mother of two sons and has three grandsons. She lives with her husband, a retired geophysicist, in Colorado.

JOHN ASHBERY
Selected Poems
Self-Portrait in a Convex Mirror

PAUL BEATTY
Joker, Joker, Deuce

JOSHUA BENNETT
The Sobbing School

TED BERRIGAN
The Sonnets

LAUREN BERRY
The Lifting Dress

PHILIP BOOTH
Lifelines: Selected Poems 1950–1999

JULIANNE BUCHSBAUM
The Apothecary's Heir

JIM CARROLL
Fear of Dreaming: The Selected
*   Poems*
Living at the Movies
Void of Course

ALISON HAWTHORNE DEMING
Genius Loci
Rope
Stairway to Heaven

CARL DENNIS
Another Reason
Callings
New and Selected Poems 1974–2004
Practical Gods
Ranking the Wishes
Unknown Friends

DIANE DI PRIMA
Loba

STUART DISCHELL
Dig Safe

STEPHEN DOBYNS
Velocities: New and Selected Poems:
*   1966–1992*

EDWARD DORN
Way More West

ROGER FANNING
The Middle Ages

ADAM FOULDS
The Broken Word

CARRIE FOUNTAIN
Burn Lake
Instant Winner

AMY GERSTLER
Crown of Weeds
Dearest Creature
Ghost Girl
Medicine
Nerve Storm
Scattered at Sea

EUGENE GLORIA
Drivers at the Short-Time Motel
Hoodlum Birds
My Favorite Warlord

DEBORA GREGER
By Herself
Desert Fathers, Uranium Daughters

God
In Darwin's Room
Men, Women, and Ghosts
Western Art

TERRANCE HAYES
Hip Logic
How to Be Drawn
Lighthead
Wind in a Box

NATHAN HOKS
The Narrow Circle

ROBERT HUNTER
Sentinel and Other Poems

MARY KARR
Viper Rum

JACK KEROUAC
Book of Blues
Book of Haikus
Book of Sketches

JOANNA KLINK
Circadian
Excerpts from a Secret Prophecy
Raptus

JOANNE KYGER
As Ever: Selected Poems

ANN LAUTERBACH
Hum
If in Time: Selected Poems,
*   1975–2000*
On a Stair
Or to Begin Again
Under the Sign

CORINNE LEE
Plenty

PHILLIS LEVIN
May Day
Mercury
Mr. Memory & Other Poems

PATRICIA LOCKWOOD
Motherland Fatherland
*   Homelandsexuals*

WILLIAM LOGAN
Macbeth in Venice
Madame X
Strange Flesh
The Whispering Gallery

ADRIAN MATEJKA
The Big Smoke
Map to the Stars
Mixology

MICHAEL MCCLURE
Huge Dreams: San Francisco and
*   Beat Poems*

ROSE MCLARNEY
Its Day Being Gone

DAVID MELTZER
David's Copy: The Selected Poems
*   of David Meltzer*

ROBERT MORGAN
Dark Energy
Terroir

CAROL MUSKE-DUKES
An Octave above Thunder
Red Trousseau
Twin Cities

ALICE NOTLEY
Certain Magical Acts
Culture of One
The Descent of Alette
Disobedience
In the Pines
Mysteries of Small Houses

WILLIE PERDOMO
The Essential Hits of Shorty Bon Bon

LIA PURPURA
It Shouldn't Have Been Beautiful

LAWRENCE RAAB
The History of Forgetting
Visible Signs: New and Selected
*   Poems*

BARBARA RAS
The Last Skin
One Hidden Stuff

MICHAEL ROBBINS
Alien vs. Predator
The Second Sex

PATTIANN ROGERS
Generations
Holy Heathen Rhapsody
Quickening Fields
Wayfare

ROBYN SCHIFF
A Woman of Property

WILLIAM STOBB
Absentia
Nervous Systems

TRYFON TOLIDES
An Almost Pure Empty Walking

SARAH VAP
Viability

ANNE WALDMAN
Gossamurmur
Kill or Cure
Manatee/Humanity
Structure of the World Compared
*   to a Bubble*

JAMES WELCH
Riding the Earthboy 40

PHILIP WHALEN
Overtime: Selected Poems

ROBERT WRIGLEY
Anatomy of Melancholy and Other
*   Poems*
Beautiful Country
Box
Earthly Meditations: New and
*   Selected Poems*
Lives of the Animals
Reign of Snakes

MARK YAKICH
The Importance of Peeling Potatoes
*   in Ukraine*
Unrelated Individuals Forming a
*   Group Waiting to Cross*